The Rhythmic Cycles
of Optimism and Pessimism

THEIR ORIGINS; THEIR EFFECTS UPON STOCK MARKET PRICES,
MONEY AND CREDIT, OTHER LEADING INDICATORS, AND PRIVATE
SPENDING; THEIR CHALLENGE TO THE RANDOM-WALK THEORY

THEIR ORIGINS; THEIR EFFECTS UPON STOCK MARKET PRICES,

MONEY AND CREDIT, OTHER LEADING INDICATORS, AND PRIVATE

SPENDING; THEIR CHALLENGE TO THE RANDOM-WALK THEORY

The RHYTHMIC CYCLES of OPTIMISM and PESSIMISM

by L. PETER COGAN

THE WILLIAM-FREDERICK PRESS

NEW YORK   1969

Library of Congress Catalog Card Number : 72-94446
Standard Book Number : 87164-103

William-Frederick Press
55 East 86th Street
New York, N. Y. 10028

Contents

Acknowledgments

THE chart and figure materials in this monograph are by the author, with the exception of Figure 3 (the Dow-Jones Industrial and Rail Averages), which is reprinted from *The Stock Picture,* published by M. C. Horsey & Co., Salisbury, Maryland 21801, with the permission of the publisher.

The two papers included in the Appendix as collateral material to the thesis of this work were written by the author in 1937 and 1959, respectively.

ABOUT THE AUTHOR . . .

AN economist, scientist, and merchandiser, L. PETER COGAN was born in Vermont and was graduated a Phi Beta Kappa from Tufts College in 1936. He received his M.B.A. degree with distinction in 1938 from the Harvard Business School, where he was a research assistant at the Bureau of Business Research. Joining the Abraham and Straus department store organization, he held various merchandising positions and served as a vice president until his retirement in 1967, when it was stated: "His unusually perceptive approach to merchandising techniques and his remarkable ability to analyze and interpret figures has given his work a very special distinction." Mr. Cogan's listings in *Who's Who in the East, World Who's Who in Commerce and Industry,* and *Leaders in American Science* note several research papers he has authored and his membership in numerous economic and scientific professional societies. Mr. Cogan resides in New York City.

The Rhythmic Cycles
of Optimism and Pessimism

THEIR ORIGINS; THEIR EFFECTS UPON STOCK MARKET PRICES,
MONEY AND CREDIT, OTHER LEADING INDICATORS, AND PRIVATE
SPENDING; THEIR CHALLENGE TO THE RANDOM-WALK THEORY

ALTHOUGH it is generally accepted that stock market prices reflect recurring alternations of optimism and pessimism to a considerable degree, most authorities are of the opinion that no clear evidence has been presented to indicate that stock market prices and/or optimism and pessimism tend to repeat themselves in cycles of approximately the same form and/or duration. Many attempts have been made to show a periodicity of business cycles, that is, a definite time interval from peaks to troughs, peaks to peaks, and troughs to troughs. None of these has stood up over a long period of time. The various lengths that have been presented have had the character of averages rather than of mechanical periodicity. On the other hand, current economic theory does not adequately explain the major and unexpected turning points in business and consumer sentiment.[1]

After thirty years of empirical observation and correlation—inspired by the late Joseph Snider, my professor in the course on business conditions

analysis at the Harvard Graduate School of Business Administration; by the pioneering studies of Arthur F. Burns, Wesley C. Mitchell, and Geoffrey H. Moore at the National Bureau of Economic Research; by Elmer C. Bratt's *Business Cycles and Forecasting* (1937); by Harold T. Davis' *The Analysis of Economic Time Series* (1941) for the Cowles Commission for Research in Economics; and by Edward R. Dewey's extensive comparative cycle research for the Foundation for the Study of Cycles—I have discovered rhythmic (that is, reasonably regular) cyclical patterns of optimism and pessimism on a yearly basis from 1870 to 1968.

A Challenge to the Random-Walk Theory

The aim of this monograph is to present these rhythmic cycles and to show that private borrowing, major business contractions, various leading indicators, and especially stock market prices (a very sensitive and volatile leading indicator of business activity) appear to follow these rhythmic cycles of optimism and pessimism to a remarkable

---

1. My paper, "Favorable and Unfavorable Factors in the Business Outlook and Their Influence on Business Confidence," November 26, 1937, at the Harvard Business School (see Appendix A), impelled me to search for new explanations for the changes in confidence.

degree in timing, sequence, and amplitude tendency. This phenomenon indicates that changes in direction and degree from optimism to pessimism, and vice versa, are not wholly chance or random behavior. It challenges the random-walk theory of stock market prices and implies that to a considerable extent stock market cycles and the persistent fluctuations of the United States economy have a psychological origin that is rhythmic.

An Important Aid to Fiscal and Monetary Decision-Makers

Knowledge of the rhythmic pattern of turning points in optimism and pessimism, especially after it has been refined to a monthly or even to a quarterly basis, could be an important aid to the proper application of fiscal action and monetary management. Economic policy decisions require the forecast of a number of economic variables, but the most difficult and important variables to forecast are expenditures in the private sector of the economy, i.e., business investment in plant, equipment, and inventories, and consumer spending for durable goods. In both of these categories the direction of future expenditures is based upon both the ability to spend and the willingness to borrow, lend, and spend. The current and future willingness to borrow, lend and spend is in a large measure dependent upon the psychological factor of optimism or confidence. Consequently, a rhythmic cyclical pattern of optimism and pessimism that is nonrandom throws new and revealing light on turning-point theory, on forecasting problems, and on monetary and fiscal policies for economic growth and stability. Further economic-scientific research needs to be directed toward their causation in order to refine the rhythmic cycles to a quarterly or monthly basis and to validate projections of the rhythmic patterns into the future.

1

The Ideal Rhythmic Cycles of

Optimism and Pessimism, 1870-1969

Chart 1,A Shows the Ideal Timing

Chart I,A presents the *ideal* timing of the cycles of optimism and pessimism from 1870 to 1968. The solid lines indicate the years when the cycles are in the "positive" phase; the dotted lines indicate the years when the cycles are in the "reverse" or "negative" phase.

The "Positive" Phase

An analysis of Chart I,A indicates that an "ideal" 17-year timing pattern for the positive phase (from late 1888 to the middle of 1950) appears to be as shown in Figure 1, when the long-term trend has been removed. For example, the 1915-32 pattern is indicated in Figure 1 (*The Ideal Timing Pattern in the Positive Phase*).

The ups and downs follow this pattern for 17 years and then repeat themselves (up approximately 1 year, down 1 year, up 2 years, down 2 years, up 2 years, down 2 years, up 1 year, down

1 year, up 2 years, and down 3 years). Each peak and each trough has a corresponding peak and trough approximately 17 years apart. Consequently, the 3-year decline from 1929 to 1932 repeats itself 17 years later, from 1946 to 1949, and 17 years earlier, from 1912 to 1915. Within an ideal 17-year period, as indicated in Figure 1 and Chart I,A, the troughs tend to appear at intervals of approximately 2, 4, 4, 2, and 5 years apart; the peaks are 3, 4, 3, 3, and 4 years apart. Note the 5-year interval between the troughs of 1910-15, 1927-32, and 1944-49, each 17 years apart.

The "Negative" or Reverse Phases

The ideal timing pattern for late 1873 to early 1888 and for late 1950 to early 1966 (Chart I,A, dotted lines) appears in the reverse or negative phase with that of the late 1888 to the middle of the 1950 period. The reversals take place during late 1873 to the negative, early 1888 to the posi-

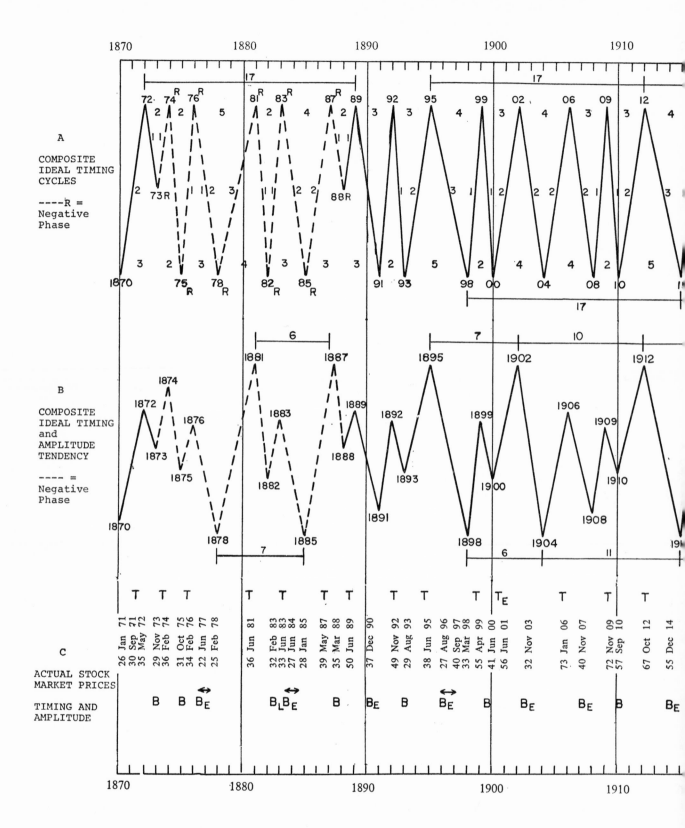

Source: 1871-1897 (Cowles Index – All Stocks, Monthly Average
         1897-1968 (Dow Jones Industrials: 1897-1929, Monthly Average;
                    1930-1968; H.-L. Monthly).

[14]

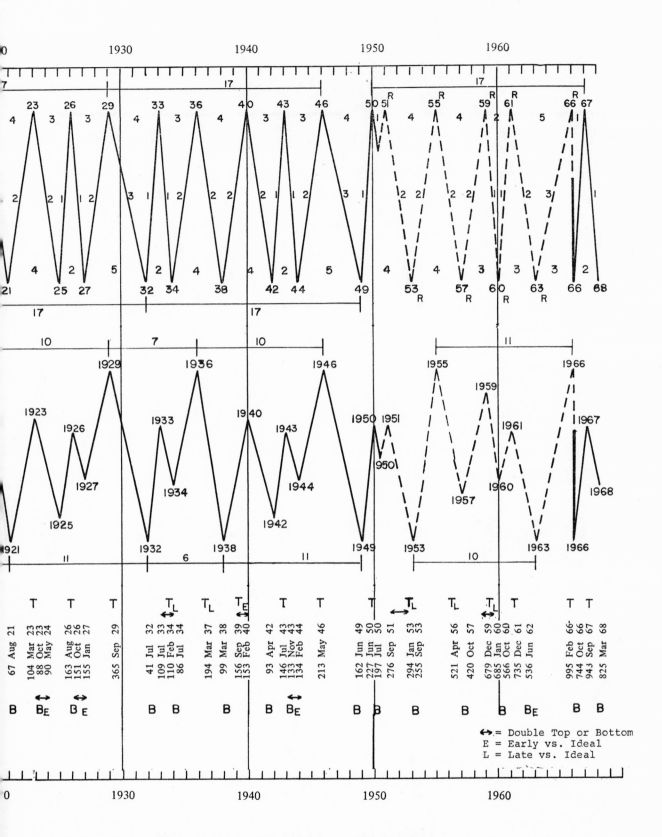

*Chart I.   The Rhythmic Cycles of Optimism and Pessimism, 1870-1968,
and Stock Market Prices, 1871-1968*

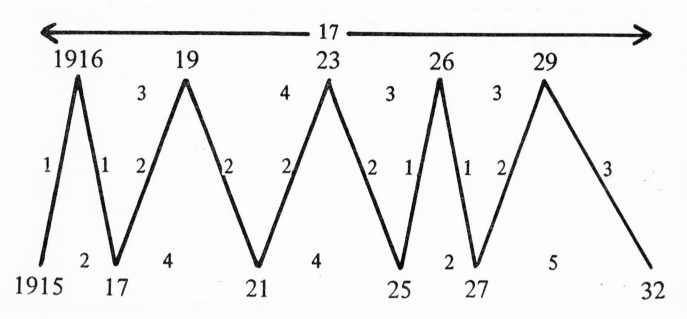

Figure 1.   The Ideal Timing Pattern in the Positive Phase, 1915-32

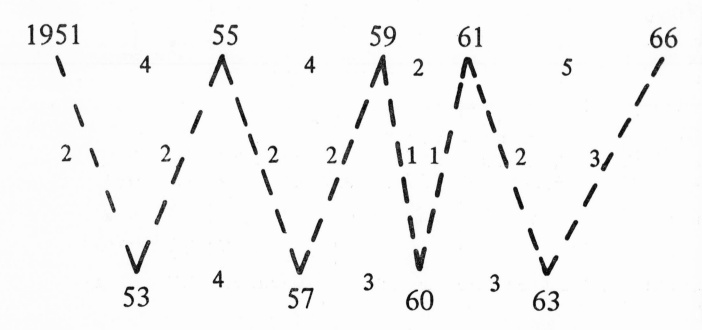

Figure 2.   The Ideal Timing Pattern in the Negative Phase, 1951-66

[16]

tive, the middle of 1950 to the negative, and late 1966 back to the positive phase. For example, the reverse or negative pattern for 1951 to early 1966 is indicated in Figure 2 (*The Ideal Timing Pattern in the Negative Phase*).

Note that the 1951 peak is equivalent to the 1934 trough in reverse, 17 years earlier, i.e., a peak becomes a trough, and vice versa: 1953 as 1936, 1955 as 1938, 1957 as 1940, 1959 as 1942, 1960 as 1943, 1961 as 1944, 1963 as 1946, and early 1966 as 1949, but in reverse.

The "Positive" Phases Again

The ideal timing patterns for late 1870, 1871, 1872, and early 1873, and late 1966, 1967, and 1968, are in the positive phase, similar to the late 1888 to the middle 1950 period. Late 1966 is a trough in timing like 1932, 1967 is a peak like 1933, and 1968 is like 1934. Since the reversal takes place in 1966, the year 1966 is both a major peak and a trough year, and this could account for the 1966 credit crisis year.

The 40-41- Month Cycle

This ideal cycle pattern of optimism and pessimism explains the so-called "40-41-month average" stock market cycle. For example, during the 17 years from 1915 to 1932 there were five cycles for an average of 3.4 years (or 40.8 months) each; however, as indicated above, the ideal cycle ranged from approximately 2 years to 5 years. In other words, there is no 40-41 month cycle; 40-41 months (or 3.4 years) are merely the averages of the 2- to 5-year cycles over a period of 17 years (as shown in Figure 1).

The "Decennial Pattern"

This ideal cycle discovery also explains the failures and coincidental successes of the "decennial pattern" theory of stock prices discovered by Edgar Lawrence Smith and followed by some stock market analysts. When the decennial pattern has been in phase with the rhythmic cycles, it has been successful, but when it has been out of phase, as in 1949, it has failed.

Chart 1,B Shows the Ideal Timing and Amplitude Tendency

Chart I,B shows the ideal timing and amplitude tendency of the rhythmic cycles of optimism and pessimism. An analysis of Chart I,B indicates that in the 1888-1950 period the ideal major declines start in 1895, 1912, 1929, and 1946. Also, the ideal large declines start in 1902, 1919, and 1936. At the other extreme, the ideal minor declines start in 1892, 1909, 1926, and 1943. Somewhat more important are the ideal declines that start in 1899, 1916, 1933, and 1967 and the declines from 1889, 1906, 1923, and 1940.

Major Turning Points at 7- and 10- or 6- and 11-Year Intervals

The major ideal peaks of optimism in the positive phase tend to appear at alternating intervals of 7 and 10 years, i.e., 1895-1902 (7 years), 1902-12 (10 years), 1912-19 (7 years), 1919-29 (10 years), 1929-36 (7 years), and 1936-46 (10 years).

The major ideal troughs in the positive phase are 6 and 11 years apart, i.e., 1915-21 (6 years),

1921-32 (11 years), 1932-38 (6 years), and 1938-49 (11 years).

In the reverse or negative phase the major ideal peaks are 6 and 11 years apart and the major ideal troughs are 7 and 10 years apart, i.e., peaks 1881-87 (6 years) and 1955-66 (11 years); troughs 1878-85 (7 years) and 1953-63 (10 years).

The interval between three major peaks or three major troughs, as shown in the positive phase, is 17 years: 10 plus 7 (17 years), 11 plus 6 (17 years).

The Timing of the Next Phase Reversal

Recent research findings, based upon the period prior to late 1870 (not shown in the charts), indicate that the ideal rhythmic cycle should change from the positive phase to the negative phase near the beginning of 1969. Consequently, this should result in an important stock market decline in 1969 and also a decline, first, in the "leading indicators" and then in the rate of growth of the "concurrent" and "lagging" indicators of business activity.

The 1/4 and 1/12 of 17-Year Ideal Rhythmic Cycles in Stock Market Prices

In addition to the ideal cycles that average 1/5 of 17 years (3.4 years, or 40.8 months), as shown in Charts I,A and I,B, there are also strong indications since 1949 (not shown on the charts) of ideal average cycles of 1/4 of 17 years (4 1/4 years, or 51 months) and, since 1966 (not shown on the charts), of ideal average cycles of 1/12 of 17 years (1 5/12 years, or 17 months).

The 1/4 of 17-year cycles (51 months) for the 17-year period from 1949 to 1966 have ideal major bottoms in the middle of 1949, late in 1953, late in 1957, in the middle of 1962, and late in 1966. The ideal bottom of the 1/5 of 17-year cycles is in early 1963. This single conflict may explain the double bottom in 1962.

The 1/12 of 17-year cycles (17 months) from 1966 to 1968 have an ideal top early in 1966, a bottom late in 1966, a top near the middle of 1967, a bottom early in 1968, and a top very late in 1968. An ideal bottom is indicated after the middle of 1969.

2

A Comparison of Actual Stock Prices, 1871-1968,

With the Ideal Rhythmic Timing Patterns

of Optimism and Pessimism

The Timing of Actual Stock Price Tops and Bottoms

Chart I,C shows the actual tops and bottoms of stock prices (1871-1968). The letter T indicates the year of the top and B the year of the actual bottom; E indicates that the actual top or bottom comes earlier than the ideal date; and L indicates that it comes later. This chart identifies the month of the top and the bottom, and the price.

The Actual Versus the Ideal Tops and Bottoms

Chart II,A is a summary of the actual versus the ideal tops and bottoms in the positive phases.

1. Out of a total of 21 tops, 2 actual tops are earlier than the ideal, 2 are later, and 17 are on schedule. Of the early tops, one is in the first part of the prior year (June 1901 versus the ideal 1902) and one is in the latter part of the prior year (September 1939 versus the ideal 1940). Both late tops are in the early part of the following year (February 1934 versus the ideal 1933 and March 1937 versus the ideal 1936).

2. Out of a total of 20 bottoms, 8 are early, none are late, and 12 are on schedule. However, of the 8 early bottoms, 6 are in October-December of the prior year, but 2—1923 and 1896—are two years early.

3. Many of the actual major tops seem to come in the latter part of the year—1919, 1929, 1936 (March 1937), and 1946. Many actual major bottoms seem to come in the early part of the year, such as in 1938, 1942, and 1949. This tendency may help to explain the 6 bottoms that come 1 to 3 months prior to the ideal bottom year and tends to indicate the need for further research to determine the exact month or quarter of the ideal top and bottom; the ideal pattern that is shown is an approximate one since it indicates the cycles only on a yearly basis.

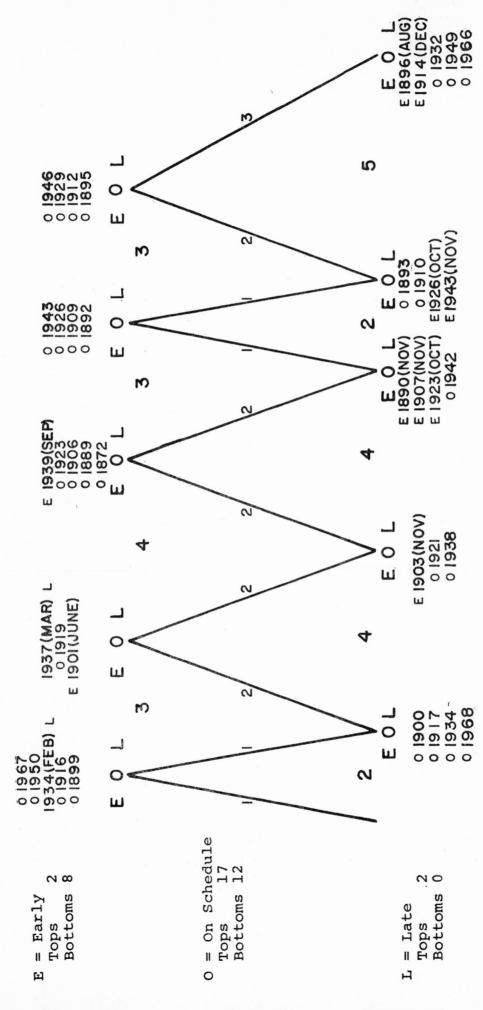

Chart IIA. *Actual Versus Ideal Tops and Bottoms in Stock Market Prices—Positive Phase*

E = Early
Tops 2
Bottoms 8

O = On Schedule
Tops 17
Bottoms 12

L = Late
Tops 2
Bottoms 0

E O L
o 1967
o 1950
1934(FEB) L
o 1916
o 1899

E O L
3

1937(MAR) L
o 1919
E 1901(JUNE)

E O L
4

E O L
4

E 1939(SEP)
o 1923
o 1906
o 1889
o 1872

E O L
3

E O L
2

E O L
1943
o 1926
o 1909
o 1892

E O L
3

E O L
2

E O L
o 1946
o 1929
o 1912
o 1895

E O L
5

E O L
o 1900
o 1917
o 1934
o 1968

E O L
2

E 1903(NOV)
o 1921
o 1938

E 1890(NOV)
E 1907(NOV)
E 1923(OCT)
o 1942

E O L
4

o 1893
o 1910
E 1926(OCT)
E 1943(NOV)

E O L
2

E 1896(AUG)
E 1914(DEC)
o 1932
o 1949
o 1966

[20]

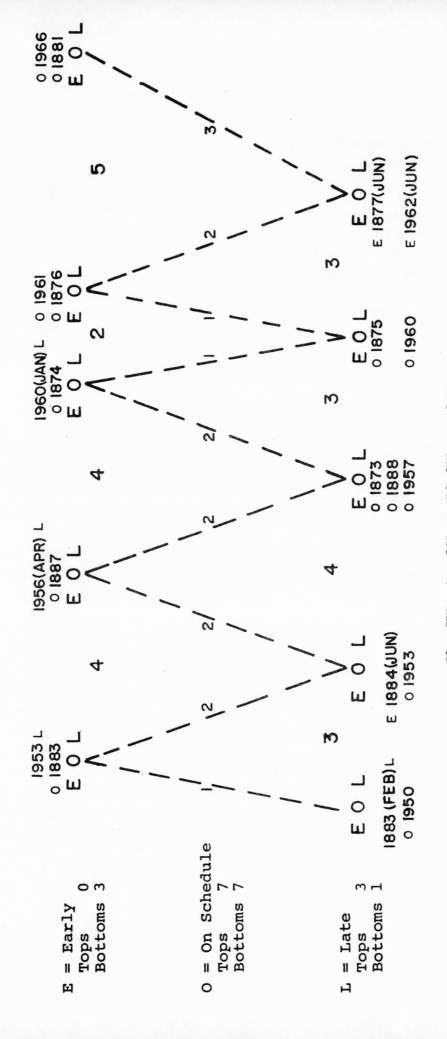

Chart IIB. Actual Versus Ideal Tops and Bottoms in Stock Market Prices—Negative Phase

Chart II,B is a summary of the actual versus the ideal tops and bottoms in the negative phases.

1. Out of a total of 10 tops, 3 are late, none are early, and 7 are on schedule. Two late tops occur in the early part of the following year (April 1956 versus the ideal 1955 and January 1960 versus the ideal 1959). One double-tops in 1951-53.

2. Out of 11 bottoms, 7 are on schedule, 1 is late, and 3 are early. The 3 early bottoms are all in the prior June (1884, 1887, and 1962). In the 1951-66 period the on-schedule bottoms tend to come late in the year (1953, 1957, and 1960).

In the period 1871-1968 there are 62 actual turning points; 43 are on schedule versus the ideal, 13 are early, and only 6 are late; out of 31 tops, 24 are on schedule.

These figures demonstrate a relatively high degree of correlation, especially when it is recognized that no stock market index can be a perfect reflection of the ideal rhythmic cycles of optimism and pessimism. Moreover, it is possible that there could be a closer correlation if we knew the exact monthly or quarterly timing of the ideal rhythmic cycles.

Major Turning Points at 7- and 10- and 6- and 11-Year Intervals

The actual major tops in the long positive phase appear at alternating intervals of approximately 7 and 10 years; the interval between the 3 major tops is 17 years.

1895-June 1901	6 1/2 years (approx.)
June 1901-1912	10 1/2 years (approx.)
1912-1919	7 years
1919-1929	10 years
1929-March 1937	7 1/4 years (approx.)
March 1937-1946	9 3/4 years (approx.)

Actual major bottoms in the long positive phase appear at alternating intervals of approximately 6 and 11 years (except 1896-1903); the interval between the 3 major bottoms is 17 years.

1896-November 1903	7 years (approx.)
November 1903-December 1914	11 years
December 1914-1921	6 years (approx.)
1921-1932	11 years
1932-1938	6 years
1938-1949	11 years

In the negative phase the major tops are 1881-87 (6 years) and April 1956-66 (approximately 10 instead of the ideal 11 years); the major bottoms are 1877-84 (approximately 7 1/2 years) and 1953-62 (approximately 9 plus versus the ideal 10 years). In the short negative phases the regularity of the intervals between the stock market major tops and bottoms is inconclusive.

During the entire 1871-1968 period the widest deviation appears in the 1896 bottom versus the ideal of 1898. The ideal 3-year drop from optimism to pessimism from 1895 to 1898 produced a business crisis that started in 1895, but apparently the greatly increased production of gold reversed the trend in late 1896. This would indicate that strong monetary factors are able to modify the ideal timing and amplitude cycle.

A Comparison of Actual Stock Prices With the Ideal Timing Amplitude Pattern

A comparison of Charts I,B and I,C shows that the actual amplitude of major declines in 1895, 1912, and 1946 in the positive phase follows the ideal pattern. However, the actual 1929-32 drop is much larger than anticipated. In the negative phase the actual large advances up to 1881 and up to 1966 follow the ideal pattern.

Also, the actual declines follow the ideal declines from 1902, 1919, and 1936 reasonably well, as do the advances to 1887 and to 1955. At the other extreme, the actual declines are minor, as indicated by the ideal patterns in 1909, 1926, and 1943, but are larger than expected in 1892. At the next level there are moderate declines in 1899, 1933, 1950, and 1967, but the drop from 1916 to 1917 is larger than the ideal pattern.

Until we find another possible cause, we must attempt to explain the larger than the ideal declines in 1892, 1916, and 1929 in terms of prior excess stock market speculation and various fiscal and monetary factors.

It is well accepted that the amplitude of business and stock market cycles is, to a large extent, influenced by monetary and fiscal policies. However, it is interesting to note the influence of multiples of 17 years. The extreme boom high of 1929, in the positive phase, is 51 years (3 times 17) from the major depression bottom of 1878 in the negative phase, and the extreme bottom of 1932, in the positive phase, is 51 years after the major top of 1881 in the negative phase. Moreover, perhaps it is no coincidence that the 1967-68 gold crisis was 34 years (2 times 17) after the 1933-34 gold crisis.

3

A Comparison of the Actual Prices of a Cyclical

Stock, TWA, With the Ideal Time-Amplitude

Pattern of Optimism and Pessimism

An inspection of Chart III (Trans-World Airlines, Inc.) shows how a so-called cyclical stock follows the ideal pattern of optimism and pessimism (Chart I,B) from 1932 to 1968, years which include the positive and negative phases of the rhythmic cyclical patterns.

The Actual Versus the Ideal Timing of Tops and Bottoms

In the positive phase, 1932, 1933, 1934, and 1936 are on schedule; there is a double bottom in late 1937 and in early 1938 versus the ideal 1938; 1940, 1942, and 1943 are on schedule; there is a double bottom late in 1943 and in early 1944 versus the ideal 1944; the top comes in December 1945 instead of in the ideal 1946; a double bottom comes in late 1948 and in early 1949 versus the ideal 1949; there is a top in early 1950 and the beginning of a decline in 1950 on schedule.

In the negative phase from late 1950 to early

1966 the actual follows the ideal pattern every year except in 1963, when the actual bottom came in 1962 as a double bottom in June and October. In this so-called cyclical stock we see clearly the tops in 1951 and 1955, which are not so clearly apparent in the Dow Jones Industrial Index.[1] In 1966 the stock tops early in the year on schedule and drops into October 1966, when the ideal pattern reverses back to the positive phase for late 1966, 1967, and 1968. TWA makes a bottom in late 1966, a top in 1967, and a bottom in 1968 (March) on schedule.

The Actual Versus the Ideal Timing-Amplitude Tendency

The amplitude of the actual prices follows the ideal pattern rather closely in both the positive and negative phases. There are major bottoms in

1. See Figure 3.

[24]

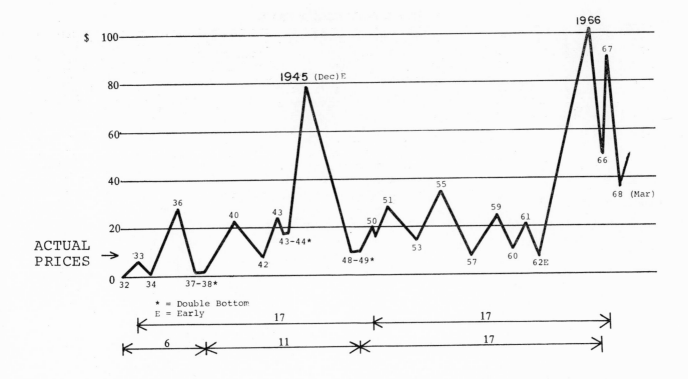

ACTUAL PRICES →

* = Double Bottom
E = Early

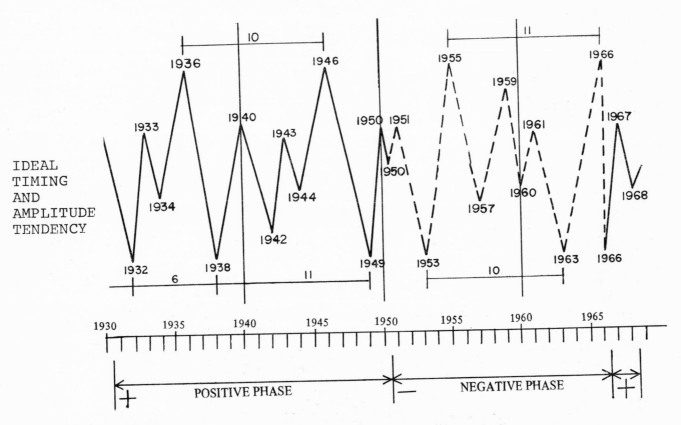

IDEAL TIMING AND AMPLITUDE TENDENCY

POSITIVE PHASE   NEGATIVE PHASE

Chart III. Trans-World Airlines, 1932-68, Versus the Ideal Pattern

[25]

DOW-JONES INDUSTRIAL AVERAGE

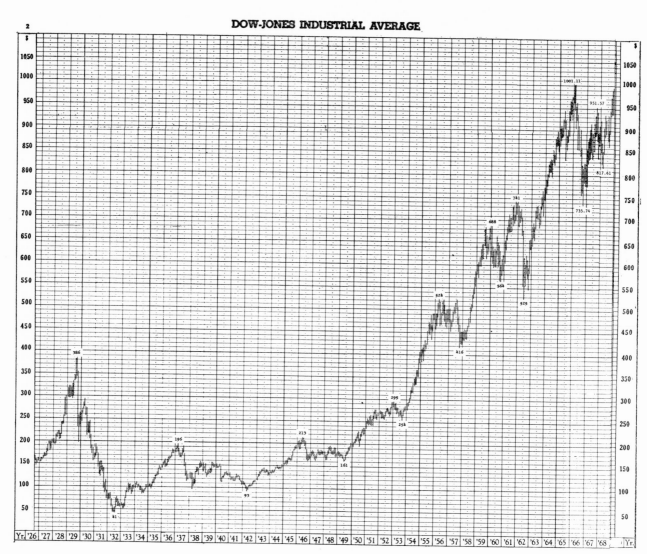

DOW-JONES RAIL AVERAGE

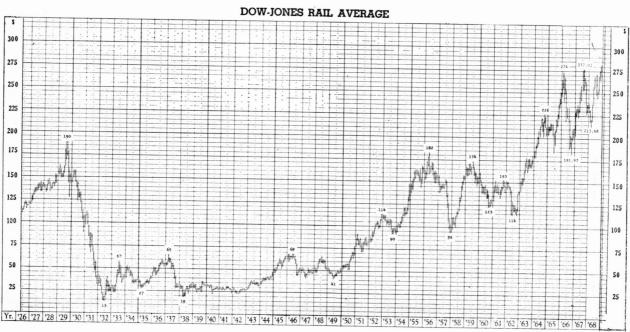

Figure 3.

1932, 1938, November 1948 versus the ideal 1949, 1953, and 1962 versus the ideal 1963, and major tops in 1936, December 1945 versus the ideal 1946, 1955, and 1966.

In the positive phase the major bottoms are approximately 6 and 11 years apart (1932-1938-November 1948); the major tops are approximately 10 years apart (1936-December 1945), as in the ideal pattern. In the negative phase, the major top of 1955 is approximately 6 years after the positive phase bottom of November 1948 and 11 years before the early 1966 top, as in the ideal pattern. The major bottom of 1953 is approximately 7 years after the positive top of December 1945, but 9 years before 1962, instead of the ideal 10 years, since the 1962 bottom is early

versus the ideal 1963; however, this was a major TWA bottom.

Rhythmic Investor Psychology a Major Factor

On the whole, it appears that the ideal rhythmic cycles reflect changes in optimism and pessimism as they affect cyclical stocks. Consequently, a cyclical stock, such as TWA, follows the ideal pattern more closely than mixed averages, such as the Dow, Standard and Poor's, etc. The high degree of conformity of the actual TWA price pattern to the ideal pattern seems to indicate rather strongly that stock price cycles are not random events. It also confirms the premise that investor psychology is a major factor in the cyclical motion of stock prices.

[27]

4

The Random-Walk Theory of Stock Market Prices
and the Rhythmic Cycles of Optimism and Pessimism

The close correlation of both aggregate stock market prices and TWA stock prices with the rhythmic cycles of optimism and pessimism seems to refute the random-walk theory of stock price changes. This theory, first proposed by Bachelier,[1] implies that speculative prices fluctuate randomly about their intrinsic values and that historical data about the price of a stock or stock prices are of little help in forecasting future prices.

The random-walk hypothesis assumes an approximate Brownian motion, according to Osborne,[1] and states that the next move is independent of all past moves and that, therefore, knowledge of past price changes yields no significant information about future price changes. Roberts[1] infers that seemingly regular patterns are illusory and are the result of pure chance. However, Alexander[1] concludes that there are "trends" in stock market prices if the "move" is taken as the unit rather than "time." Granger and Morgenstern[1] find, through spectral analysis, that while the simple random-walk model explains rather well the short-run movements of the stock prices, the model does not adequately explain the very important long-run movements. In fact, they find some evidence of a forty-month cycle, but only inconclusively, as one would expect from my prior comments on this cycle. The impression that one gets from the Cootner[1] selection of essays is that while the simple random-walk model does not fully describe the movements of stock prices, in modified form it is considered to be a reasonable approximation.

The rhythmic cycles of optimism and pessimism, at this stage, offer no theory or pattern for short-run movements, but they have produced empirical evidence that would seem to refute the random-walk hypothesis for long-run movements of stock prices.

————————

1. Cootner, Paul H. (ed.), *The Random Character of Stock Market Prices*. Cambridge, Massachusetts: The M.I.T. Press (1964).

5

The Money Supply, the Major Business

Contractions, and the Ideal Rhythmic

Cycles of Optimsm and Pessimism

Discussing money and business cycles, Friedman and Schwartz[1] state: "The outstanding cyclical fact about the stock of money is that it has tended to rise during both cyclical expansions and cyclical contractions . . . . The only major exceptions since 1867 to the tendency of the money stock to rise during both cyclical expansions and cyclical contractions occurred in the years listed in the following tabulation, which gives also the percentage decline during each exception.

Years of Exception	*Percentage Decline*
1873-79	4.9
1892-94	5.8
1907-08	3.7
1920-21	5.1
1929-33	35.2
1937-38	2.4

"In addition, there were two minor exceptions since the end of World War II:

1948-49	1.4
1959-60	1.1

The major exceptions clearly did not fall in a random subset of years. Each corresponds with an economic contraction that was major as judged by the other indicators; in the period covered there was no other economic contraction more severe than any in the list."

Friedman and Schwartz therefore conclude that the decline in the money stock was a major cause of the contraction in business activity in the periods listed.

In reply to this and subsequent papers by the Chicago School, Davis[2] states: "There is a real question as to whether anything can be inferred

---

1. "Money and Business Cycles," *The Review of Economics and Statistics* (February 1963).

2. Davis, R. G., "The Role of the Money Supply in Business Cycles," Federal Reserve Bank of New York *Monthly Review* (April 1968).

from the historical record about the influence of money on business if, as is argued in the next section, there is an important reverse influence exerted by the business cycle on the monetary cycle itself . . . . The fact that the business cycle itself has an important role in determining the course of the monetary cycle seriously undermines the argument that the timing relationships of monetary cycles and business cycles point to a dominant influence of money on business. By the same token, ample room is left for the possibility that many other factors, such as fiscal policy, fluctuations in investment demand, including those related to technology, fluctuations in exports, and replacement cycles in consumer goods, may also exert independent influences on the course of business activity."

Rhythmic Cycles
the Missing Links

I suggest that the rhythmic cycles of optimism and pessimism are the "missing links" and were an important factor in the business contraction periods listed by Friedman and Schwartz. *Every money and business contraction listed by Friedman and Schwartz and every advance from those declines were triggered by a rhythmic cycle change from optimism toward pessimism, and vice versa,* as indicated on Chart I,B (*Ideal Timing and Amplitude Cycles*), as follows:

Years of Exception	Years of Ideal Cycle Decline
1873-79	1872-73
	1874-75
	1876-78
1892-94	1892-93
1907-08	1906-08

1920-21	1919-21
1929-33	1929-32
1937-38	1936-38
1948-49	1946-49
1959-60	1959-60

This empirical evidence would tend to support the proposition that while the money supply has an influence on business and business on money supply, the rhythmic cycles of optimism and pessimism influence speculation and business expectations; "lack of confidence" adversely affects the willingness to lend, borrow (Chart IV, *Ideal Cycles vs. Money and Credit*), and spend on business investment and consumer durables, can lead to panics and runs on banks, and can precipitate major stock price declines. It therefore supports the "Keynes and Simons interpretations of 1929-33: they both argued that it is a collapse of confidence which sets off a demand for liquidity, that this demand cannot be met but the attempts to meet it force liquidation, and that this liquidation includes bank loans with a resultant decline in the quantity of money . . . . both Simons and Keynes emphasized the state of business expectations and the desire for liquidity."[3]

Moreover, the remarkable time correlations of money, business, and the rhythmic cycles during the years listed by Friedman and Schwartz are a further confirmation of the reality of the rhythmic cycles of optimism and pessimism.

Furthermore, this new theory is consistent with the findings of Anderson and Jordon[4] that a change in Z is explained by factors other than monetary and fiscal forces, where Z is a variable

---

3. Davis, J. Ronnie, *American Economic Review* (June 1968).
4. Anderson, Leonall C., and Jordon, Jerry L., "Monetary and Fiscal Actions: A Test of Their Relative Importance in Economic Stabilization," Federal Reserve Bank of St. Louis *Review* (November 1968).

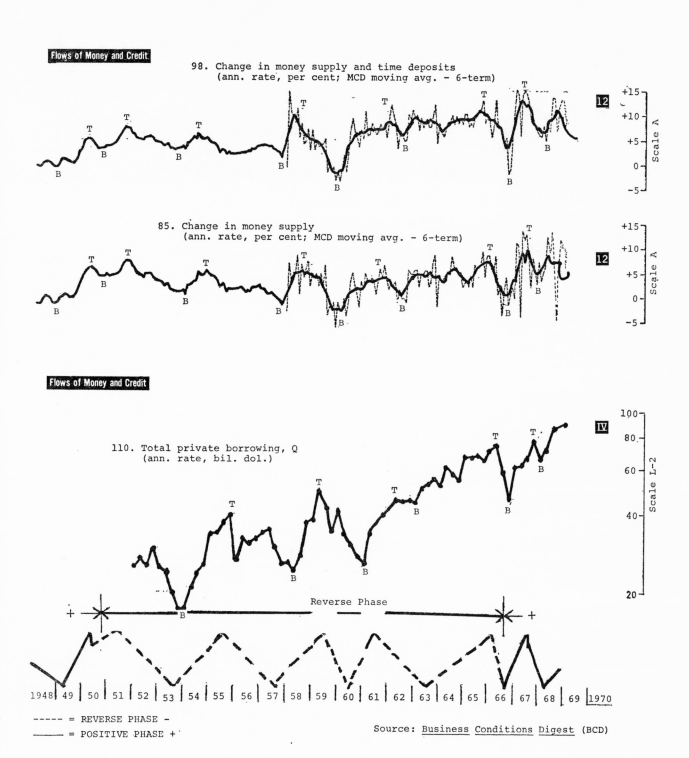

98. Change in money supply and time deposits
(ann. rate, per cent; MCD moving avg. - 6-term)

12

Scale A

85. Change in money supply
(ann. rate, per cent; MCD moving avg. - 6-term)

12

Scale A

IV

Scale L-2

110. Total private borrowing, Q
(ann. rate, bil. dol.)

Reverse Phase

1948 49 50 51 52 53 54 55 56 57 58 59 60 61 62 63 64 65 66 67 68 69 1970

----- = REVERSE PHASE -
——— = POSITIVE PHASE +

Source: Business Conditions Digest (BCD)

TIMING OF IDEAL CYCLES (yearly basis)

Chart IV. Ideal Cycles Versus Money and Credit

summarizing all "other" forces that influence total spending. Their major conclusions are that fiscal actions have little influence upon total spending unless the deficit is financed by an increased money supply, but that changes in the money supply are a major influence. However, since it has already been shown that changes in the cycles of optimism and pessimism influence demand-induced changes in the money supply, the findings of Anderson and Jordon furnish additional evidence for the large role of the rhythmic cycles of optimism and pessimism on private spending.

6

Some Leading Business Indicators
and the Ideal Rhythmic Pattern

The sensitive "Leading Business Indicators" (1948-68), as published in the Department of Commerce *Business Condition Digest* (formerly *Business Cycle Developments*), seem to correlate with the ideal rhythmic pattern in the positive and the negative phases to a degree that cannot be explained by chance or random behavior. The following *BCD* volatile series are suggested for comparison:

Series 1. *Average Workweek, Production Workers, Manufacturing* (hours). (Chart V.)

In the positive phase, 1949 is a bottom and on schedule versus the ideal cycle; there is a rise into the middle of 1950; and the start of a decline on schedule.

In the reverse phase, there is a rise from the middle of 1950 to a top in 1951 on schedule; a bottom very early in 1954 versus the ideal 1953; a top in 1955 on schedule; a bottom very early in 1958 versus the ideal 1957; a top in 1959 and a bottom in 1960, both on schedule; a top in early 1962 versus the ideal 1961; and a bottom in late 1963 and a top in early 1966, both on schedule.

In the positive phase, there is a bottom very early in 1967 versus the ideal late 1966; and a top in 1967 and a bottom in early 1968, both on schedule. The major discrepancy is in 1952.

Series 6, *New Orders, Durable Goods Industries* (bil. dol.). (Chart V.)

In the positive phase, 1949 is a bottom on schedule versus the ideal cycle; there is a rise into the third quarter of 1950 and the beginning of a decline on schedule.

In the reverse phase, there is a rise to a top in 1951 on schedule; a bottom in September 1953 and a top in December 1955, both on schedule; a bottom in January 1958 versus the 1957 ideal; a top in 1959 on schedule; a bottom in January 1961 versus the ideal 1960; a top in early 1962 versus the ideal 1961; a bottom in 1962 versus the ideal 1963; and a top in late 1966 versus the ideal early 1966.

In the positive phase, there is a bottom in early 1967 versus the ideal late 1966; a top in January 1968 versus the ideal 1967; and a bottom in 1968 on schedule.

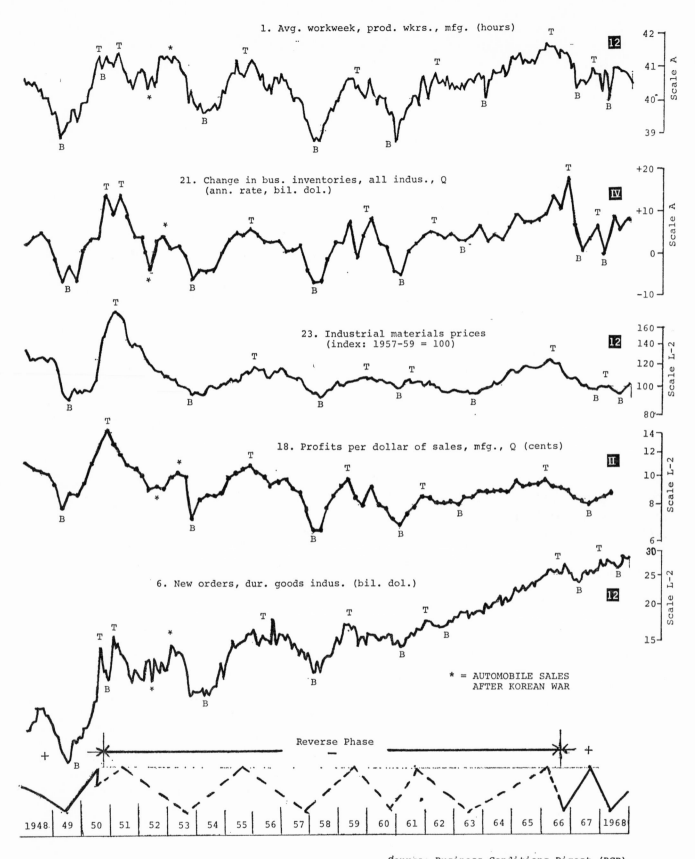

1. Avg. workweek, prod. wkrs., mfg. (hours)

21. Change in bus. inventories, all indus., Q
(ann. rate, bil. dol.)

23. Industrial materials prices
(index: 1957-59 = 100)

18. Profits per dollar of sales, mfg., Q (cents)

6. New orders, dur. goods indus. (bil. dol.)

* = AUTOMOBILE SALES
AFTER KOREAN WAR

Reverse Phase

1948 | 49 | 50 | 51 | 52 | 53 | 54 | 55 | 56 | 57 | 58 | 59 | 60 | 61 | 62 | 63 | 64 | 65 | 66 | 67 | 1968

Source: Business Conditions Digest (BCD)

TIMING OF IDEAL CYCLES (yearly basis)

Chart V. Ideal Cycles Versus the Leading Indicators

[34]

Series 21 (now Series 245), *Change in Business Inventories, All Industries,* Q. (ann. rate bil. dol.). (Chart V.)

In the positive phase, there is a bottom in 1949 on schedule; a rise into 1950; and the beginning of a decline on schedule.

In the negative phase, there is a top in 1951, a bottom in 1953, and a top in 1955, all on schedule; a bottom very early in 1958 versus the ideal 1957; a double top in 1959 and early 1960 (because of the steel strike) versus the ideal 1959; a bottom very early in 1961 versus the ideal 1960; a top in the first quarter of 1962 versus the ideal 1961; a bottom in 1963 on schedule; and a top in late 1966 versus the ideal early 1966.

In the positive phase, there is a bottom in the second quarter of 1967 versus the ideal late 1966; and a top in 1967 and a bottom in the first quarter of 1968, both on schedule.

Series 23, *Industrial Materials Prices* (Index: 1957-59=100). (Chart V.)

In the positive phase, there is a bottom in 1949 on schedule; a slight rise into 1950; and a plateau through early 1950.

In the negative phase, there is a rise to a top in 1951 on schedule; a bottom in February 1954 versus the ideal 1963; a top in December 1955 on schedule; a bottom in April 1958 versus the ideal 1957; and a top in 1959, a bottom in 1960, a top in 1961, a bottom in 1963, and a top in early 1966, all on schedule.

In the positive phase, the bottom is in 1967 versus the ideal late 1966; a slight rise to a top in both 1967 and early 1968; and a bottom in 1968, as with the ideal.

Series 18, *Profits per Dollar of Sales, Manufacturing,* Q. (cents). (Chart V.)

In the positive phase, there is a bottom in 1949

and a sharp rise into 1950 on schedule; however, there is no start of a decline in 1950.

In the reverse phase, there is a sharp rise to a peak in the fourth quarter of 1950 versus the ideal 1951; a bottom in 1953 and a top in 1955, both on schedule; a bottom in the first quarter of 1961 versus the ideal 1960; a top in 1961, a bottom in 1963, and a top in the first quarter of 1966, all on schedule.

In the positive phase, there is a bottom in 1967 versus the ideal late 1966, and a continuation of the rise without a dip from 1967 into 1968. However, in Series 16, *Corporate Profits After Taxes,* Q. (ann. rate, bil. dol.), there is a bottom in the first quarter of 1967 versus the ideal late 1966, and a top in the fourth quarter of 1967 and a bottom in the first quarter of 1968, both on schedule.

In Series 1, 21, 18, and 6, the 1952-53 distortion is not forecast by the ideal cycle. It was caused by the sharp drop in automobile sales from 1950 to 1952 during the Korean War and then by the sharp rise from 1952 to 1953 (see Series 234, *Automobile Sales,* and Series 113, *Change in Consumer Installment Debt*).

Money and Credit
Reflect Rhythmic Cycles

Special attention is again directed to Series 85, *Change in Money Supply,* Series 98, *Change in Money Supply and Time Deposits,* and Series 110, *Total Private Borrowing* (Chart IV), in view of the many recent articles on the role of the money supply in business cycles. These series follow the ideal rhythmic pattern to such a high degree that it would seem that the ideal rhythmic cycles of optimism and pessimism influenced the timing of cycles in private borrowing and in the demand-induced money supply; the turning points in money are generally earlier because of the monetary moderating action by the Federal Reserve. While "changes" in money supply had an influence upon business and business upon the demand-induced money supply, it is seen here that the rhythmic cycles of optimism and pessimism had an important influence upon expectations and upon the timing and amplitude of private borrowing and business. On the other hand, it would appear that fiscal and monetary policy influenced the amplitude and timing of the money supply and then the business cycles in varying degrees, depending upon the action taken and the confidence, liquidity, and ingenuity of the lenders, borrowers, and spenders. Perhaps prior knowledge of the ideal rhythmic cycles could have avoided the unnecessary sharp changes in monetary and fiscal action during 1966, 1967, and 1968.

What Happens When Rhythmic Cycles Reinforce or Oppose Fiscal and Monetary Action

In view of the degree of correlation between the leading business indicators and the ideal cycles, it is suggested that the long rhythmic cycle of optimism from 1963 to 1966 was a major factor in the 1963-66 boom, in addition to the important tax measures and monetary expansion. Moreover, the rise of the ideal cycle of optimism from its early 1968 bottom explains the 1968 advance of stock prices and the "unexpected" sustained high in consumer spending and, especially, in business lending, borrowing, and spending through the spring of 1969, despite the influence of the tax surcharge, high interest rates, and a tight monetary, fiscal, and debt management policy.

It seems that we must conclude that the business cycle still exists in the private sector and that stock prices and both consumer and businessmen's expectations, spending, borrowing, and bank lending are influenced by changes in optimism and pessimism that are rhythmic in nature.

In fact, at the same time that optimism and pessimism influence stock prices, major stock price changes, as an early indicator and through realized and "paper" profits and losses, in turn influence and reinforce expectations, spending, borrowing, and lending both upward and downward.

Business Depressions, Emotional Depressions, and the Rhythmic Cycles of Pessimism

It is also interesting to note that psychiatric research indicates a correlation between business depressions and the peak periods of emotional depressions and the rhythmic cycles of pessimism. Brenner[1] finds that fluctuations in mental hospital admissions show strong inverse correlations with fluctuations in the employment index in New York State over the period 1910 to 1960. Therefore, since it has been shown that both employment and economic activity show a strong positive relationship to the ideal rhythmic cycles of pessimism, we have evidence here for the speculation that the rhythmic cycles of pessimism are related to both emotional and business depressions.

Consequently, more knowledge about the rhythmic cycles of optimism and pessimism should improve the proficiency in economic forecasting,

---

1. Brenner, M. H., "Economic Change and Mental Hospitalization: New York State, 1910-1960," *Social Psychiatry,* 2:4 (1967).

which is so important for any "New Economics." Moreover, this knowledge would be valuable for longer forecasts of 3 to 5 years; most present methods are not designed for this objective. While structural and institutional changes in the United States economy seem to have made the business cycle more stable since 1946, there is no certainty of a continuation of stability in the future.

7

The Possible Origins of the

Rhythmic Cyclical Patterns

The Overlapping Rhythmic Cycles and the Timing of Reversals

The ideal composite timing and amplitude cycles (Chart I,B) seem to be a synthesis of overlapping rhythmic cycles that produce the rise and decline in terms of time and amplitude and trigger the turning points. Chart VI,A,B (*Overlapping Rhythmic Cycles and Timing of Reversals*) illustrates the ten overlapping rhythmic cycles, each with tops and bottoms 17 years apart. The letter R on Chart VI indicates when the cycle is in the reverse or negative phase, shown reversed as dotted lines on Chart I,A,B. Chart VI,A, lines 1-5, show, on a yearly basis, the timing, duration, and amplitude tendency of declines in the positive phase and advances in the R or negative phase. Chart VI,B, lines 1-5, show, on a yearly basis, the timing, duration, and amplitude tendency of advances in the positive phase and declines in the R or negative phase.

Declines in the Positive Phases and Advances in the Negative Phases

Chart VI,A, line 1, in the positive phase, shows on a yearly basis the ideal declines of one year from 1899 to 1900, 1916 to 1917, 1933 to 1934, and 1967 to 1968. Since 1950 is a reversal year, it is both a top and a bottom. In the negative R phase, line A1, 1882 to 1883 becomes an advance; likewise, 1950 to 1951 in the R phase is an advance.

A2, in the positive phase, shows the major ideal declines of three years from 1895 to 1898, 1912 to 1915, 1929 to 1932, and 1946 to 1949. In the negative R phase, 1878 to 1881 and 1963 to 1966 become major ideal advances.

A3, in the positive phase, shows the ideal declines of two years from 1889 to 1891, 1906 to 1908, 1923 to 1925, and 1940 to 1942. In the positive phase, 1872 to late 1873 is a decline. In the R phase, 1874 becomes a top after a rise from

1873, the reversal year; likewise, in the R phase, 1957 to 1959 becomes an advance.

A4, in the positive phase, shows the major ideal declines of two years from 1902 to 1904, 1919 to 1921, and 1936 to 1938. In the R phase, 1885 to 1887 and 1953 to 1955 become major ideal advances.

A5, in the positive phase, shows the ideal declines of one year from 1892 to 1893, 1909 to 1910, 1926 to 1927, and 1943 to 1944. In the R phase, 1875 to 1876 and 1960 to 1961 become advances.

Each 1-, 2-, or 3-year movement is followed by a 16-, 15-, or 14-year movement to complete a 17-year cycle.

Advances in the Positive Phases and Declines in the Negative Phases

Chart VI,B, line 1, in the positive phase, shows on a yearly basis ideal advances of one year from 1891 to 1892, 1908 to 1909, 1925 to 1926, and 1942 to 1943. In the R phase, 1874 to 1875 and 1959 to 1960 become declines.

B2, in the positive phase, shows the ideal major two-year advances from 1893 to 1895, 1910 to 1912, 1927 to 1929, and 1944 to 1946. In the R phase, 1876 to 1878 and 1961 to 1963 become declines.

B3, in the positive phase, shows the ideal one-year advances from 1898 to 1899, 1915 to 1916, 1932 to 1933, 1949 to 1950, and late 1966 to 1967. In the R phase, 1881 to 1882 becomes a decline.

B4, in the positive phase, shows the ideal two-year advances from 1900 to 1902, 1917 to 1919, and 1934 to 1936. In the R phase, 1883 to 1885 becomes a decline.

B5, in the positive phase, shows the ideal two-year advances from 1870 to 1872, 1904 to 1906, 1921 to 1923, and 1938 to 1940. In the R phase, 1887 to early 1888 is a decline, since 1888 is a reversal year. In the positive phase, 1888 to 1889 is an advance.

The major ideal tops of 1895, 1912, 1929, and 1946 are in the same series (A2), each 17 years apart. The major ideal bottoms of 1898, 1915, 1932, and 1949 are in the same series (B3), each 17 years apart. The major tops of 1902, 1919, and 1936 are in the same series (A4). The major bottoms of 1904, 1921, and 1938 are in Series B5. In the R phase, tops become bottoms, and vice versa. The major ideal tops of 1881 and 1966 and the major ideal bottoms of 1878 and 1963 are in the same series (A2).

The many repetitions and correlations of the ideal and actual cycle patterns in terms of timing, duration, and amplitude tendency in the positive and negative phases would seem to point to non-random causes. This thesis is also supported by the fact that the 1873-88 reverse-phase pattern returns in the same timing form in the 1950-66 reverse-phase period. Moreover, the cycles of optimism and pessimism tend to persist and correlate to a high degree, regardless of war or peace or technological changes over a period of nearly a hundred years.

Emotions of Optimism and Pessimism May Be Influenced by Solar System

Medical-space research will be required to determine the exact mechanisms by which the emotions of optimism and pessimism are influenced; however, we can speculate that changes in electromagnetic forces or other changing patterns of

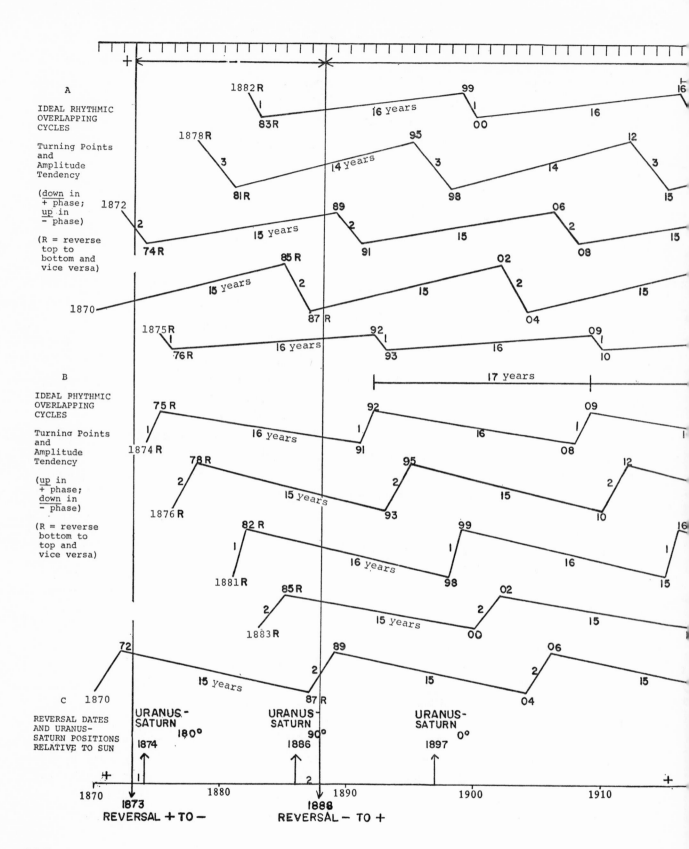

A

IDEAL RHYTHMIC
OVERLAPPING
CYCLES

Turning Points
and
Amplitude
Tendency

(down in
+ phase;
up in
− phase)

(R = reverse
top to
bottom and
vice versa)

B

IDEAL RHYTHMIC
OVERLAPPING
CYCLES

Turning Points
and
Amplitude
Tendency

(up in
+ phase;
down in
− phase)

(R = reverse
bottom to
top and
vice versa)

C

REVERSAL DATES
AND URANUS-
SATURN POSITIONS
RELATIVE TO SUN

1882R
83R
16 years
99
00
16
16

1878R
3
81R
14 years
95
3
98
14
12
3
15

1872
2
74R
15 years
89
2
91
15
06
2
08
15

1870
15 years
85 R
2
87 R
15 years
02
2
04
15

1875R
76R
16 years
92
93
16
09
10

17 years

75 R
1
1874 R
16 years
92
1
91
16
09
1
08

78 R
2
1876 R
15 years
95
2
93
15
12
2
10

82 R
1
1881R
16 years
99
1
98
16
16
1
15

85 R
2
1883R
15 years
02
2
00
15

72
1870
15 years
89
2
87 R
15 years
02
2
00
06
2
04
15

URANUS-
SATURN
180°

URANUS-
SATURN
90°

URANUS-
SATURN
0°

1874
1

1886
2

1897

1870
1880
1890
1900
1910

1873
REVERSAL + TO −

1888
REVERSAL − TO +

[40]

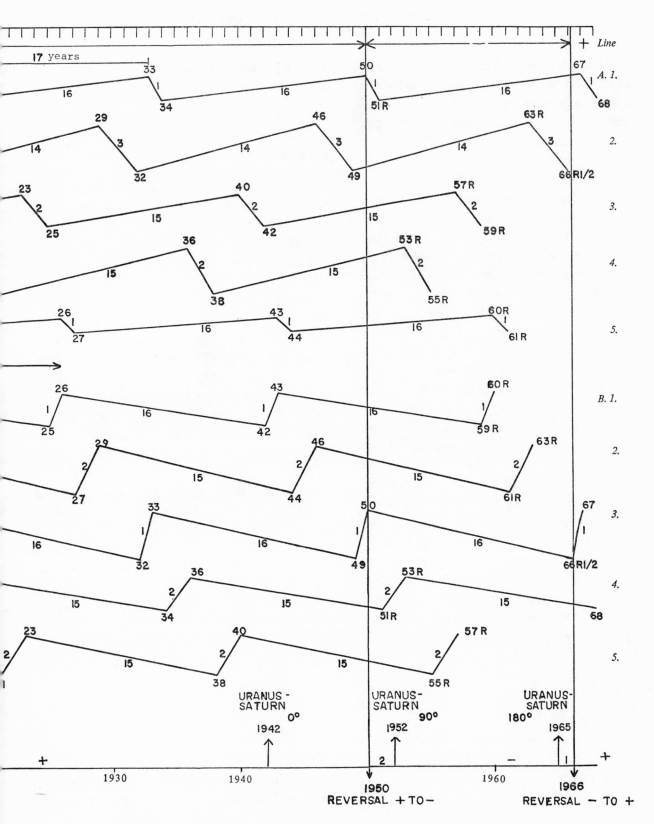

Chart VI. Overlapping Rhythmic Cycles and Timing of Reversals

[41]

solar system emissions and fields of force may be involved which could operate on the psychology of man through neurological and/or biochemical processes. It has long been known, for example, that changes in the ionization of the air can produce powerful physical, mental, and emotional effects.[1] Takata has found that the composition of human blood changes in relation to the sunspot cycle, to solar flares and sunrise, and to eclipses.[2] Jose concluded that certain dynamic forces exerted on the Sun by the motions of the planets were the cause of solar activity.[3] Bjorn, Hasseltine, and Pimm have developed techniques for the prediction of mean sunspot numbers using planetary influences.[4] Space research is discovering many planetary-solar-terrestrial relationships which may provide a key to the mechanisms involved.[5]

Many years of medical-ionization research for my paper, "Seasonal Cycles of the Common Cold and Their Relationship to Suceptibility,"[6] and my astronomy and planetary-solar-terrestrial research as a member of the American Geophysical Union and the New York Academy of Science, lead me to speculate that the rhythmic cycles may be related to the rhythmic movements of the planet Uranus relative to Saturn in their rotations around the Sun. Each of the 17-year rhythmic overlapping cycles seem to be related to the 45.36-year synodic period of Uranus and Saturn. The synodic period is the interval between two successive conjunctions (0°) of the two planets relative to the sun. The

17-year period is equivalent to almost exactly 3/8 of the 45.36 period (3/8 of 45.36 is 17.01).

Rhythmic Cycle Reversal
Dates and Uranus-Saturn Positions

The Uranus-Saturn hypothesis appears to be strongly supported by the dates of reversal from the negative to the positive phases, and vice versa (Chart VI,C, *Reversal Dates and Uranus-Saturn Positions*). The reversals in 1873, 1888, 1950, and 1966 appear to be related to the 180° and 90° positions of Uranus to Saturn relative to the Sun. As noted on Chart VI,C, the reversal in 1873 took place approximately 1 year before the Uranus-Saturn 180° position in 1874; the early 1888 reversal occurred approximately 2 years after the Uranus-Saturn 90° position of early 1886. In a similar manner, the 1950 reversal took place approximately 2 years before the Uranus-Saturn 90° position of early 1952 and the 1966 reversal occurred 1 year after the Uranus-Saturn 180° position of 1965. *In the 1870-1968 period the actual cycles and the ideal rhythmic cycles of optimism and pessimism in the positive and the negative phases appear to form a symmetrical pattern relative to the Uranus-Saturn 180° and 90° positions of 1874-86, respectively, the 0° of 1897 and 1942, and the 90° and 180° positions of 1952-65, respectively. This symmetry of the actual and ideal cycles in both the negative and positive phases tends to confirm a rhythmic pattern rather than chance or random events.*

A Major Research
Project Needed

A major scientific-economic research project is suggested to confirm this new theory; to test its

---

1. See Appendix B, "Seasonal Peaks of Common Cold Incidence and Sunspot Activity."
2. Takata, Maki, *Time Magazine* (March 21, 1969).
3. Jose, Paul D., "Sun's Motions and Sunspots," *Astronomical Journal*, 70: 3 (April 1965).
4. Bjorn, T., Jr., Hasseltine, C. C., Pimm, R. S., "Prediction of Mean Sunspot Numbers Using Planetary Influences," American Geophysical Union, Annual Meeting, 1969.
5. Gauquelin, Michel, *The Cosmic Clocks*. Chicago: Henry Regnery (1967).
6. *Journal of Cycle Research* (1955): on file in the New York Academy of Medicine.

findings versus the random-walk theory; to determine the exact quarterly or monthly turning points of the overlapping and composite cycles; and to investigate the specific cause of the 17-year patterns.

In the meantime, it will be interesting to note the degree and duration of fiscal and monetary actions that are needed to overcome and modify the influence of the timing and amplitude of the ideal rhythmic cycles of optimism and pessimism.

8

Conclusions and Implications

The relatively high degree of timing, sequence, and amplitude tendency correlations between actual stock prices, other leading business indicators, private borrowing, and major business contractions and the ideal rhythmic patterns seem to confirm the existence of rhythmic cycles of optimism and pessimism rather than chance or random events as casual factors. It seems to refute the random-walk theory of stock price changes. This new theory is supported by the long series of rhythmic 17-year patterns, as illustrated in the composite and individual overlapping rhythmic cycles in both the positive and the negative phases. It appears that the causation of these rhythmic cycles and their phase reversals is of solar system origin and may be related to the rhythmic movements of the planets Uranus and Saturn relative to each other and to the Sun.

Monetary and fiscal policies do not appear to be the primary major causes of the business cycle, but appear to modify the amplitude and, to some extent, the timing for better or worse, depending upon the correctness of their timing, the strength of the action, and the concurrent influence of the confidence, liquidity, and ingenuity of lenders, borrowers, and spenders. It would appear that 1929 and 1932 would have been major turning points regardless who had been President. Despite the importance of the influence of military and political decisions upon the economy, the business cycle in the private sector still persists.

The existence of rhythmic cycles of optimism and pessimism implies that economics is more of a science than has been recognized. It is therefore recommended that a major scientific research project be undertaken by the economic, medical, and space agencies of the federal government, in collaboration with universities and private research organizations, to determine a more accurate timing of the rhythmic cycles of optimism and pessimism and their phase reversals, and also to investigate the precise mechanism by which changes in the solar system's fields of force influence the human emotions of optimism and pessimism.

Cycle theory based upon the evidence presented here, together with further research to refine and project the cycles into the future, should be of valuable assistance in solving short- and long-range forecasting problems and in guiding fiscal action and monetary management for economic growth and stability and for a better balance between the objectives of full employment and price stability.

Appendix

Appendix A

*Favorable and Unfavorable Factors
in the Business Outlook and Their
Influence Upon Business Confidence*[1]

At the present time the status of business sentiment is the most important factor underlying the current situation. More than ever, the psychological factor is at work. Therefore, although we might speak of various favorable and unfavorable factors as though they were independent forces, it should not be overlooked that the importance of most of these factors lies in their stimulating or depressing effect upon business confidence. It should also be realized that these various factors are so closely interrelated that changes in one lead to a series of changes in many of the others.

Unfavorable Factors

Without doubt, the most unfavorable factor at present is the deeply entrenched "fear of further

decline" in the minds of businessmen. As long as this lack of confidence exists, we cannot expect capital to flow into new enterprises, or purchases of new equipment and commitments of any sort to be made.

At present we find that purchasing agents are deferring 1938 buying, awaiting a further working off of inventories, which are still high in many industries. Buying is being held to a hand-to-mouth basis. Normally, contracts for 1938 supplies are signed at this time of year, but now they are being deferred until after January 1. This is perhaps unfortunate, for these are the fellows who must start the ball rolling again. It is the purchasing agents who help keep the capital goods industries going. A high rate of production in the capital goods industries increases purchasing power for consumer goods and leads to further stimulation of capital goods.

It is thus evident that whatever might dampen

1. A paper submitted at the Harvard Business School, November 26, 1937.

the confidence of the users of capital goods is of the utmost importance. In this region we find a number of unfavorable factors. In the first place, inventories are still high, and unfilled orders are practically nil. Moreover, commodity prices, especially raw materials, are still falling. This has a tremendous psychological effect, for when prices are falling, buyers are certain to hold off, so that prices fall still farther without possibility of immediate adjustment. Thus the volume of industrial production continues to decline, and this decreases the ability of the people to buy. This is evidenced by the present decline in payroll and, thus, in purchasing power.

Furthermore, the incentive for private capital to flow into industry on a large scale is weakening. The profit margins of many corporations are narrowing as a result of high costs, especially labor, and corporate inability to raise selling prices in the face of consumer resistance to a higher cost of living. Corporations are thus hesitant now about further expansion. This hesitancy is no doubt influenced by the tax on undivided profits. The reason is obvious. A few courageous businessmen, however, are still willing to take a chance at expansion, but they find that the slump in stocks and bonds has made new financing almost impossible. Recent new flotations are finding themselves on the shelves of the investment houses.

Can hope be expected to be offered by the railroad, automobile, or building industries?

In the railroad industry, we find that recent wage increases have practically crippled most roads, despite increased rates. To this is added the reduction in income because of the falling off in carloadings. The purchase of new equipment is being definitely postponed. Moreover, the industry is laying off countless workers.

The automobile industry has been watched eagerly during the past month. Much hope for a stimulus to business was placed on this industry, for it is a huge purchaser of materials—steel, copper, glass, etc. But at the present time, we find that the automobile industry may disappoint us, for the response to the new models does not appear to be very encouraging.

In the building industry, the rate of decline is rapid. Despite a rise in rents through September, the high costs of building construction are still frightening away the speculative builders. To be sure, building is dependent to a great extent upon general business, but, at the same time, construction by builders who are confident that there is a need and a pressing demand for housing can stimulate other industries and directly and indirectly increase employment and purchasing power.

And so, steel operations are down to about 33 per cent of capacity. This low rate of operation is a depressing force, for besides resulting in unemployment and curtailment of expansion, it spreads fear to other industries. Wide fluctuations are a natural phenomenon in this industry, but this fact is not fully realized at this time.

Speaking again of confidence, we cannot overlook the stock market. Without doubt, the rapid collapse of stock prices was chiefly responsible for the sudden relapse of business sentiment. The current decline is further aggravating the situation. With reference to the stock market slump, in addition to its effect upon new financing and business sentiment in general, it is having an unfavorable effect on the will to buy of investors who are finding that their huge "paper profits" are being wiped out.

Turning to purchasing power, we find that there is a continuous decline. National income leveled off some time ago and is now drifting downward. The decline in government spending has, no doubt, been a factor. As a result, retail trade is becoming less optimistic and is not holding up to expectations. Although consumer purchasing power is mainly dependent upon industrial production, the opposite is also true.

In this area we also find that the current trend of farm income is downward as a result of declining prices of farm products.

In the realm of labor, unfavorable developments are again taking place. Strikes are again breaking out in the automobile and rubber industries. This is by no means a healthy tonic for business sentiment.

In the money and banking situation, we should not overlook the declining volume of bank credit. Although it may be an indication of the working off of inventories, it is deflationary. As long as the supply of money and credit in circulation continues to decline, there will continue to be a decline in business spending. We should also note that the effect of the recent outflow of gold is deflationary.

In the international situation, we can probably always expect something unfavorable, but at the present time there is a decline in the rate of armament expansion, with a resultant slowing down of many dependent industries. As we are now well aware, business conditions in Europe greatly concern us because of financial interrelationships and because the price of many commodities is set in the world markets.

Favorable Factors

Here again we find that the more important factors for the near-term outlook are those which directly influence business sentiment.

It is from this angle that recent government statements and actions are important. Business must have reason to feel that the administration is willing to cooperate. The actions of the President and Congress during the past week or more and in the near future may be able to turn the trend of sentiment.

Cooperation is being extended along several lines. In the first place, the President has promised the utilities that they can proceed with expansion without fear of government oppression, if they are willing to accept his theory of rate setting. It is estimated that cooperation with the utilities may release one to two billion dollars of capital expenditure. Already the New York State power companies have made plans for an outlay of $112,000,000 during the next two years. If other utilities will follow suit, the estimated expenditure will give strong impetus to industrial activity and purchasing power. It might be pointed out, however, that with the present decline in the bond market, utilities will have a difficult time trying to float new issues.

Then again, the government has agreed to modify the undistributed profits tax and perhaps the capital gains tax. Already the House Ways and Means Committee has approved changes in the undivided profits tax which will be helpful to the smaller companies. At least a start has been made. If further favorable action is taken, which appears likely, it will be extremely helpful at the present time, for it will lift some of the obstacles to expansion, particularly in the financially weak companies.

A reduction in the capital gains tax, as is intimated, would stimulate the pouring of private capital into industry. A huge store of potential spending power is now lying idle in bank vaults or in tax-free securities, waiting for the profit incentive to be strengthened.

Moreover, the President is planning to initiate

a huge housing program. It is his intention to encourage the formation of large-scale construction corporations financially strong enough to carry on mass building projects. He may also accept the responsibility for controlling building costs. As has already been indicated, this action would tend to stimulate other industries, as well as directly adding a vast number of men to the ranks of the employed. However, if the government attempts to drop relief and other expenditures to balance the budget, municipal costs will continue to rise and threaten higher real estate taxes. Also, residential building depends mainly upon general business conditions and their effect upon the would-be house owner, so that attempts to stimulate construction of housing directly may prove to be difficult.

Another favorable factor may be the intention to revive RFC lending. This would help railroads finance needed capital improvements at a time when income is very low. Also, managements are anticipating ICC permission to further raise rates to offset wage increases.

In the realm of government action, the present negotiations with Great Britain for a reciprocal trade agreement would stimulate exports.

It should be realized that it may take time for the government to actually carry out its plans, but a definite decision to act will in itself buck up business sentiment.

Turning to industry itself, we find encouragement in the fact that inventories are being worked off, because of the prompt adjustment of production to the lowered demand. This means that as soon as sentiment improves, production will quickly respond to increased demand. Also, there has been no overexpansion of production facilities in the leading industries. Furthermore, most of the leading companies are in a strong financial

position. These facts are important because they indicate that most corporations will not blindly attempt to sell their products at almost any cost in the hope of getting some contribution to overhead and preventing themselves from going under.

In the labor situation there is some hope, despite the recent outbreak of strikes. The present negotiations between the CIO and the AFL may lead to more conservative labor activities, for much of the strike activity is the result of a battle for leadership between the two organizations. The recent defeat of the CIO candidates in the Detroit elections might slightly dampen the confidence of CIO heads.

As for agriculture, there are some favorable aspects. Despite the continuous decline in the price of most farm products, farm income is still ahead of last year. As a result, it is anticipated that farmers will be in the market for an increased amount of farm equipment, clothing, etc. Furthermore, the President's desire to assist the farmer at this time may be helpful in maintaining his purchasing power.

In the security markets we find more steadiness than last month. The market has probably already overdiscounted the present decline in business. The day-to-day movements seem to be greatly dependent upon government action, which bears out our opinion that government action is now extremely important in stimulating business confidence.

The greater steadiness of the market may be partly due to the revised margin requirements. The action by the FRB indicates that Washington is greatly concerned over the unfavorable trend in securities and realizes its effect upon general business.

In the money and banking situation there are certain bright spots. Excess reserves are still large and interest rates are low, thus providing a large base for credit inflation. The rediscount rates charged by the FRB are exceedingly low; this offers some assurance against deflation. It is true that bank credit is declining rapidly, but, as has been noted, the downtrend of bank loans may be a favorable sign, indicating that business is reducing inventories. Some writers point with alarm at this decline in bank credit and consider it to be a major cause of the business decline. There is no doubt that the decline in investment holdings by the banks is deflationary, but if it continues, I believe the FRB will take steps to reverse the trend. It appears that the Federal Reserve Board will keep itself fully awake during the next few months.

As for the international situation, there is more reason for hope than for fear. The high state of tension that prevailed in Europe during the summer is gradually subsiding. Our nervousness over the possibility of a major war now is greatly abated. This is taking a great load off the minds of both the administration and businessmen.

Finally, all the members of the House and a third of the Senate face election next fall. These officeholders will attempt to do something to which they can point with pride. Such efforts would be definite action that would put the brakes on the present business decline.

Appendix B

Seasonal Peaks of Common Cold
Incidence and Sunspot Activity[1]

The phenomena of September-October and February-March peaks, on average, for both the common cold and sunspot activity appear to be related through the mechanism of ionization produced by X-radiation. The resultant decreased CO_2 absorption by the blood plasma, the acid-alkaline imbalance, and impaired oxygen consumption lower resistance and provide an environment for common cold viruses to attack.

Studies of the common cold indicate that two peaks of incidence often occur during the year—a major one, on average, between September and October, and the other between February and March. The peaks of incidence, noted in a study by Torney and Lake[2] of employees of Macy's department store in New York City, occurred in October and February. Downes[3] found a big peak in September and one in February-March among

persons of ages 19 and over as well as ages 5-18, in a study conducted in Westchester County, New York. Dingle[4] found a September peak among a Cleveland, Ohio group. On the basis of years of research, Dr. Perrin Long of the Department of Medicine of the Kings County Hospital, considers the phenomenon of the September-October and February-March peaks, rather than one continuous peak from September to March, as one of the greatest mysteries of the common cold.[5]

Studies of sunspots indicate that there are often two similar peaks—one, on average, between September-October, and the other, on average, between February-March. Clayton[6] found two maximum areas of sunspots each year for the period 1887-1938—one peak averaged between February and March and another averaged between Sep-

1. A paper for the Petco Research Laboratory, New York, July 14, 1959.
2. Torney and Lake, *Journal of the American Medical Association*, 117 (1924, 1941).
3. Downes, *Milbank Memorial Fund Quarterly*, 30 (1952).

4. Dingle, John, "A Study of Illness in a Group of Cleveland Families," *Journal of Hygiene* (January 1953).
5. Dr. Long's presentation of this mystery inspired the research for this paper.
6. Clayton, *Solar Cycles*, Smithsonian Misc. Collection, 106: 22 (1947).

tember and October. Arctowski,[7] studying sunspot numbers for the period 1874-1913, found a peak averaged in September and the next averaged in February. Hess and Huystic[8] confirm the existence of regular seasonal variations in sunspot numbers. Reports on the International Geophysical Year 1957-58 indicate that in September 1947 the intense solar activity produced auroras that could be mapped on twenty-five nights. The great auroral storm of February 10-11, 1958 was one of the most spectacular in many years. In March 1958, auroras were seen on every night except one. The "Observed Sunspot Numbers"[9] for this period show one peak in September-October 1957 and another in February-March 1958. Perhaps the sun's crossing of the equator in September and March is a factor.

The similarity of the seasonal peaks of common cold incidence and sunspot activity indicate a relationship between these two phenomena; the former appears to be caused by the latter. The mechanism of the relationship appears to be the change in ionization of the atmosphere during increased sunspot activity.

Sunspot activity produces X-rays that increase the ionization of the atmosphere. Freidman[10] and his associates at the Naval Research Laboratory discovered X-rays at times of solar flares in the lower D region of the ionosphere. His studies indicate that this X-radiation creates the increased ionization which leads to radio communication blackouts at times of intensive solar activity, while ultraviolet radiation does not. Soviet papers presented at the Fifth General Assembly of the

Special Committee for the International Geophysical Year indicate the relative abundance of positive ions as a result of sunspot activity. Tchijevsky[11] conducted a series of studies on sunspot numbers and concluded that increased electrical activity around the sunspot maxima increases the positive ionization of the air. Apparently, there is greater leakage of charged particles to the earth's lower atmosphere than is generally suspected.

Positive ionization appears to have many adverse influences. A two-year study by a research team at Northeastern Hospital, Philadelphia, headed by Dr. Igho H. Kornbluch of the hospital and Dr. George M. Piersol, dean of the University of Pennsylvania Graduate School of Medicine, indicates that when the air is charged with positive ions, there is a notable increase of discomfort in the form of fatigue, dizziness, headache, asthma, and sinusitis. They reported that negative ions have a beneficial influence. Puck and Sagik[12] have shown that viruses attach themselves to cells only when positive ions are present.

Physiologically, positive ionization affects the CO_2 absorption by the blood plasma and the acid-alkaline balance and impairs the O_2 intake and consumption. Professor John L. Worden,[13] of St. Bonaventure University, presents evidence that a positively ionized atmosphere decreases the ability of the blood plasma to combine with CO_2 and influences the acid-alkaline balance adversely. Haldene and Priestly, explaining the mechanism of the changes in rate of O_2 intake, show that the accumulation of CO_2 in the blood causes the respiratory center to be stimulated so that it sends im-

7. Arctowski, *Mem. Soci Spethoscopisiti*, 5 (1916), 98-99.
8. Hess and Huystic, *Cosmic Radiation and Its Biological Effects.*
9. *Predicted and Observed Numbers*, Department of Commerce, National Bureau of Standards, Boulder, Colorado.
10. Odishaw, Hugh, "International Geophysical Year," *Science*, 128 (December 26, 1958), 3339.

11. Dewey, Edward A., and Dakin, Edwin F., *Cycles—The Science of Prediction* (chapter 10). New York: Henry Holt (1954).
12. Puck, H. P., and Sagik, A. C. (October 1954).
13. Worden, John L. Paper to the American Society for Experimental Biology.

pulses to the muscles of respiration, causing more rapid breathing and consequently more oxygen intake; on the other hand, decreased CO_2 in the blood plasma reduces O_2 intake. The acidity-alkalinity imbalance, as well as low CO_2 content, influences oxidation adversely. Gray[14] confirms this O_2 phenomenon. Peterson[15] shows that the pH changed and the CO_2 content was low two days before the onset of the common cold.

Adequate O_2 intake and unimpaired oxidation are essential for adequate heat production to avoid a thermal imbalance, the green light for possible common cold viruses to attack. In my paper, "Seasonal Cycles of the Common Cold and Their Relationship to Susceptibility,"[16] it is shown that the common cold viruses apparently strike or develop when a thermal imbalance develops. This imbalance lowers resistance and provides an environment for the common cold viruses to attack. In-

creased sunspot activity, by decreasing oxygen consumption, therefore, tends to increase susceptibility to the common cold viruses. This explains the similar peaks of incidence.

This relationship of the common cold to sunspot activity throws some light on the mysteries of the common cold. It may also indicate other interrelationships of phenomena in the upper atmosphere and terrestrial events; for example, the severe influenza epidemic in the fall of 1957 and the winter of 1958 coincided with the high 1957-58 sunspot activity.

Postscript, March 1969

(1) The Hong Kong flu epidemic of 1968-69 coincided with the high 1968-69 solar activity.

(2) Since the Apollo 7 and 9 astronauts broke out with colds during the high sunspot activity in October 1968 and in February 1969, my common cold research findings are being evaluated by the chief of the Astronauts' Clinic, NASA Manned Spacecraft Center.

14. Gray, John S., "The Multiple Factor Theory of Respiratory Regulation," Project 386, Report 2: *Uncompensated Metabolic Disturbance of Acid-Base Balance,* A.A.F. School of Aviation Medicine (December 14, 1945).
15. Petersen, William F., *The Patient and the Weather.* Ann Arbor, Michigan: Edwards Brothers (1938).
16. *Journal of Cycle Research,* 4:3 (July 1955), 63-72.

NOTES

NOTES

NOTES

NOTES

NOTES

NOTES

NOTES

NOTES